IMAGES
of America

SEA BRIGHT

IMAGES
of America

SEA BRIGHT

Holly Bianchi
Foreword by Jo-Ann Kalaka-Adams

ARCADIA
PUBLISHING

Copyright © 2008 by Holly Bianchi
ISBN 978-0-7385-5762-5

Published by Arcadia Publishing
Charleston SC, Chicago IL, Portsmouth NH, San Francisco CA

Printed in the United States of America

Library of Congress Catalog Card Number: 2007935343

For all general information contact Arcadia Publishing at:
Telephone 843-853-2070
Fax 843-853-0044
E-mail sales@arcadiapublishing.com
For customer service and orders:
Toll-Free 1-888-313-2665

Visit us on the Internet at www.arcadiapublishing.com

I dedicate this book to my "Earth Angels at Summertime,"
who every day light the candles in my life.

CONTENTS

Acknowledgments   6

Foreword   7

Introduction   9

1.   Birth of a Sea Jewel   11

2.   The Place to Be by the Sea   43

3.   Beautiful Sea Bright   89

ACKNOWLEDGMENTS

I want to begin the acknowledgments by saying how grateful I am to have Mayor Jo-Ann Kalaka-Adams present the foreword for this book. As I complete this book, I want to acknowledge mayor-elect Maria Fernandes and wish her good luck. I want to say a very special thank-you to Bill Judge of the Image Shop in Red Bank and to Jeff Siegel for scanning the rare and beautiful photographs for this book. More thank-yous go to Monmouth County historian George H. Moss Jr., Frieda Finegan, Ann Early, pastor Robert J. Long of the United Methodist Church of Sea Bright, Adelina Fernandes, Lois Sommers, Nancy Burchardt, George A. Brown, Paul Boyd, Gloria Hennessey, Bill Longo, Barbara Booz, Mo Cuocci, Jim Lindemuth, Tony Mac, Jimmy Cousins, Carl Wilson, Colleen McGowan, Glen and Helen McDonough, Sterling and Fern Foster, Doris Painter, Joe and Donna Hilcken, Millie Kube, Jeanne Gough, Eleanor Milland, Bill Stephenson, Tina Kearney, Sybil Wiehl, Barbara Thornberry, Tina Bivona, Gail Gammon, Gail Turegano, John Cowie, Lorenzo de Stefano, Michele Farlow, Cynthia Bianchi, Victoria Pasko, Barbara Markey Pasko, Anne Morganthal, Paddy Miller, Robyn Bianchi Cullum, Richard Sass, George and Karen Harquail, David Johns, Laura Poll and Joan Walsh, Gateway Press, Fairbanks Inn Resort and Marina, Driftwood Beach Club, McCloone's Rum Runner, Gaiter's Bar and Grill, the J. W. Ross Library and Cultural Center, the Sea Bright Fire Department, Atlantic Highlands Historical Society, the Thomas Varne Museum and Library, the Monmouth County Historical Association Library and Archives, the Monmouth Beach Cultural Center, the *Sea Bright SeaBreeze*, the *Monmouth Journal*, and the *Two River Times*.

There is a sad ending to the acknowledgments. On February 20, 2007, Debra Lyn Yuhasz died after suffering serious injuries from a fire at the Fountain's Condominiums on February 5, 2007. Yuhasz was a native of Ohio but made Sea Bright her beloved home. I give my condolences to her family.

FOREWORD

Since 2003, I have been both happy and privileged to serve as the mayor of Sea Bright. I am also proud to have the opportunity to write the foreword to this book, which recounts Sea Bright's fascinating history in a series of rare photographs.

In the late 19th and early 20th centuries, Sea Bright was known as a "Jewel by the Sea" with its beautiful hotels that lined Ocean Avenue and exquisite restaurants that became the trademark of this mecca by the sea. Prominent businessmen made Sea Bright one of the most prosperous and beautiful seaside towns in which to live. Some of the "cottages" that they built still stand today.

A native of Wappinger Falls, New York, I and my husband, Jim, have lived here for 30 years and have watched Sea Bright continue to grow as a desirable town in which to live. I brought my brothers Billy and Michael and sister-in-law Fran to Sea Bright (their condominium was destroyed in the Fountain's fire.) My sister Jacqueline vacationed here with me for years. Now my husband is in the process of relocating his business to Sea Bright. Sea Bright has truly become a family affair for us.

Sea Bright can boast of its practically zero percent crime rate, a highly qualified police department, and a totally dedicated volunteer fire department and first aid squad. Under my watch, Sea Bright is one of the very few towns that has never exercised its eminent domain option on residents' homes and hopefully never will. Sea Bright continues to thrive and grow and be "the place to live." Looking forward, I have proposed a 40-foot-wide boardwalk for our downtown beach area, to run from Chapel Hill Beach Club to Donovan's Reef Restaurant. It would include a large Victorian-style lifeguard station and hidden cell tower, along with a skate park, benches, children's park, and possible pool. It will truly be the focus and a destination point for Sea Bright.

In the mid-1990s, Sea Bright underwent beach replenishment, where the beaches were expanded with sand, snow fences were installed, and dune grass was put on the beaches. Since then, Ocean Avenue has not experienced as much flooding during major storms. Sea Bright can be very proud of how it takes care of its environment. That is mainly due to its beautification committee and especially senior Sea Bright resident Ralph Clauer and the many hours he has spent pulling weeds, watering and planting flowers, and just simply caring about our beautiful town.

Sea Bright has had its share of tragedy throughout the years. The most recent fire at the Fountain's Condominiums, the biggest in Sea Bright history, brought out the best in Sea Bright as a community. Its firefighters, as they have many times before, showed their bravery and skill in putting out a fire despite freezing temperatures and unbearable conditions. The firemen, Ladies Auxiliary, first aid squad, and emergency management all worked tirelessly until this fire was out. If ever there was a time for the community to pull together, this was the time, and I am proud to say that both businesses and residents came to the assistance of all involved.

As mayor of Sea Bright, I look forward to a future here that continues to be as bright and beautiful as our natural setting. There is no doubt that Sea Bright is the place to live and be—it is that small, just over three miles, strip of land between our beautiful river and our fabulous sea.

Jo-Ann Kalaka-Adams
Mayor of Sea Bright

INTRODUCTION

Sea Bright is a town that began as a fishermen's village of Scandinavian immigrants and was known as Nauvoo. Later it became known as a seaside resort of the New Jersey shore, and it still remains today a popular seaside town.

Putting together *Sea Bright* was a gratifying experience both professionally and personally. Professionally I enjoyed collecting the images and other material from both Sea Bright residents and family members of those residents who once occupied this great seaside town. Personally all the happy memories of spending summers at my family's summer home on Ocean Avenue came back to me: playing on the ocean beach on warm summer days and swimming in the river, whereupon my sisters and I would take the rowboat to the sandbar and enjoy walking on it. My father would take us on boat rides on his boat, which he docked in the water behind our house, along the beautiful Shrewsbury River, and on the Fourth of July, my sisters, cousins, and I would watch the fireworks and wave sparkles at the same time. There was "amateur hour," which was held outside our house where my sisters, cousins, and I would dress up in colorful costumes and give a performance. Mine was a star-spangled costume, and I would sing "Mickey Mouse," which came from the popular Mickey Mouse Mouseketeers television show. These glorious memories and the fantastic people of Sea Bright helped me relive them. Hopefully the reader will have the same experience in the following chapters to appreciate the magnificent seaside town of Sea Bright.

One

BIRTH OF A SEA JEWEL

The history of Sea Bright goes back to the days when it was simply known as Nauvoo, a Hebrew name, when it was a quaint fishing village of the mid-1800s. In this chapter, the reader will be presented with rare photographs of Sea Bright in the 20th century, such as its highly skilled fire department, which in 1891 put out one of the biggest fires in Sea Bright history; the Long Branch and Seashore Railroad and the Jersey Central Railroad lines that provided service to many a passenger; and the Sea Bright School, the alma mater of generations of Sea Bright children.

Sea Bright in the 20th century faced many great storms. There was the devastating storm of 1914 that literally destroyed houses to pieces and washed away two streets that were behind the famous Peninsula House Hotel. There was also the 1962 storm, which damaged not only Sea Bright but much of Monmouth and Ocean Counties, and the most recent storm, the "storm of the century," the 1992 nor'easter, which traumatized Sea Bright and the surrounding towns. Sea Bright is a jewel, a rare jewel, between the Atlantic Ocean and Shrewsbury River and will forever remain that way.

Shown is a photograph (around 1900) of the Sea Bright Post Office located on Ocean Avenue. Today the post office remains on Ocean Avenue. (Courtesy of Daniel Hennessey.)

This is an early-1900s photograph of the depot of the Long Branch and Seashore Railroad at Sea Bright. Today the depot is no longer in existence; it was removed in December 1945. (Courtesy of Daniel Hennessey.)

Pictured is a 1948 advertisement for the Jersey Central Railroad lines, which provided a year-round, all-rail service going from Jersey City and Newark to the Highlands, Sea Bright, and East Long Branch. The last passenger timetables that were issued for train service to Sea Bright and East Long Branch via Matawan was on June 24, 1945, which showed 11 southbound trains and 9 northbound trains, running five days a week, Monday to Friday. (Courtesy of Bill Longo.)

Time Table in effect June 26. 1922.

Central Railroad of New Jersey.

SANDY HOOK ROUTE.

Leave S. Bright.	Arr. Pier 10 Cedar St.	Ar. Pier 81 42d St.
6.29 a. m. 6.44 a. m.	8.20 a. m.	8.40 a. m.
7.42 a. m. 7.52 a. m.	9.25 a.m.	9.45 a. m.
10.19 a. m. 10.29 a. m.	12.00 m.	12.20 p. m.
1.12 p. m. 1.19 p. m.	2.50 p. m.	3.10 p. m.
2.12 p. m. 2.24 p. m.	3.50 p. m.	4.10 p. m.
5.30 p. m. 5.42 p. m.	7.15 p. m.	7.35 p. m.

SUNDAYS.

7.34 a.m.	9.15 a. m.	9.35 a. m.
10.49 a. m. 10.59 a. m.	12.30 p. m.	12.50 p. m.
1.24 p. m. 1.35 p. m.	3.05 p. m.	
5.35 p. m.	7.00 p. m.	
8.16 p. m.	9.45 p. m.	10.05 p. m.

ALL RAIL ROUTE. Via Matawan.

Lv. S. Bright.	Ar. Liberty St.	Ar. W. 23d St.
5.58 a. m.	8.02 a. m.	8.32 a. m.
6.27 a. m.	8.32 a. m.	8.53 a. m.
7.12 a. m.	9.10 a. m.	9.25 a. m.
11.42 a. m.	2.02 p. m.	2.22 p. m.
12.23 p. m.	4.00 p. m.	4.17 p. m.

Time Table in effect June 26, 1922.

Central Railroad of New Jersey.

SANDY HOOK ROUTE.

Lv. Pier 81 42d St.	Lv. Pier 10 Cedar St.,	Ar. S. Bright
8.45 a. m.	9.10 a. m.	10.36 a. m. 10.44 a. m.
9.50 a. m.	10.15 a. m.	11.41 a. m. 11.49 a. m.
12.30 p. m.	1.00 p. m.	2.26 p. m. 2.37 p. m.
3.45 p. m.	4.10 p. m.	5.38 p. m. 5.49 p. m.
4.55 p. m.	5.20 p. m.	6.47 p. m. 6.56 p. m.
7.45 p. m.	8.10 p. m.	9.44 p. m.

SUNDAYS.

9.00 a. m.	9.30 a. m.	10.57 a. m. 11.05 a. m.
10.00 a. m.	10.30 a. m.	11.57 a. m. 12.05 p. m.
1.00 p. m.	1.30 p. m.	3.06 p. m.
	3.15 p. m.	4.51 p. m.
	6.45 p. m.	8.14 p. m. 8.29 p. m.

ALL RAIL ROUTE. Via Matawan.

Lv. W. 23d St.	Lv. Liberty St.	Ar. Sea Bright.
	3.30 a. m	7.19 a. m.
	5.30 a. m.	8.45 a. m.
8.05 a. m.	8.15 a. m.	10.21 a. m.
11.15 a. m.	11.30 a. m.	1.33 p. m.
1.00 p. m.	1.15 p. m.	3.13 p. m.
3.25 p. m.	3.40 p. m.	6.13 p. m.

Shown is a June 26, 1922, Jersey Central Railroad train schedule going the Sandy Hook route, arriving and leaving Sea Bright on weekdays and Sundays. (Courtesy of Monmouth County historian George H. Moss Jr.)

The Jersey Central Railroad, with the magnificent cottages in the background, is depicted in this postcard labeled "C. R.R. of N. J. Station at Train Time. Seabright, N. J." On August 17, 1911, at 7:00 a.m., Olef Icliadessefer wrote Florence Martinius of Stockton, "Received your postal and hi — Thanks awfully. It is hot here today but a sea-breeze is coming here and it will soon be cool. I hope you have a good time on the farm but do be careful of that (or rather those) that I sent to you. Yours Olef Icliadessefer."

This postcard titled "Highland Station, Highlands, N.J." (around 1920) depicts the time when the Highland Station ran into Sea Bright. In the background is the Highlands Bridge, which crossed into Sea Bright.

14

Shown here are fishing boats along the beach at Sea Bright, which was inhabited largely by fishermen in the early days. Sea Bright was famous as a fishermen's town. (Courtesy of Daniel Hennessey.)

This is an old remaining hut where one of Sea Bright's fishermen once lived. This hut is located on the east side of Ocean Avenue.

This early-1900s photograph shows the Sandy Hook Coast Guard station, located in the Highland Beach section of Sea Bright. From left to right are Walsh Hennessey, Milt West, George West, Capt. Joel Wooley (seated), Joe Riddle, Edgar Clayton, Holms Riddle, and an unidentified man. (Courtesy of Daniel Hennessey.)

As this storm hits a Sea Bright oceanfront home, notice the volatility of the waves. Sea Bright has suffered many storms like this one over the last 100 years. (Courtesy of Daniel Hennessey.)

This is a 1914 photograph of the aftermath of the famous hurricane that hit Sea Bright and the human devastation that resulted from this horrific storm. (Courtesy of Daniel Hennessey.)

Shown is a spectacular aerial high-tide winter view of Sea Bright along Ocean Avenue. Note the beautiful "cottager" mansions. (Courtesy of Daniel Hennessey.)

This photograph from around 1900 shows two fishermen at the entrance of what is today known as Sea Bright, which one enters after crossing the Highlands Bridge. At the time of this photograph, Sea Bright was known as Highland Beach. In the background, one can see the famous Highlands Twin Lights. (Courtesy of Daniel Hennessey.)

Shown in this 1900 photograph, 16 members of the Sea Bright Fire Department are, from left to right, Will Armstrong, George Congden, George Hainey, H. Thorsen, Cure Howland, Frank Covert, Al Stocen, Addice Howland, Nat Johns, John Howland, Evert Van Bunt, John Mount, Allie Bocker, Dan Pappinger, George Leurs, and George Conover. The firemen are in front of a half-drawn ladder trunk. The Sea Bright Fire Department was founded in 1881. (Courtesy of the Sea Bright Fire Department.)

Members of the Sea Bright Fire Department meet at the firehouse around 1910. (Courtesy of the Sea Bright Fire Department.)

In 1955, one of Sea Bright's oldest landmarks, Zobel's Boatyard, located on Ocean Avenue, caught on fire in the middle of the night. It was one of Sea Bright's largest and most well-known fires. Today condominiums stand in its place. (Courtesy of the Sea Bright Fire Department.)

This late-1950s photograph of a Sea Bright First Aid Squad fund-raiser shows Mayor Thomas Farrell (left) handing a donation to Capt. Ed Phieffer. Behind Captain Phieffer is Jack Ryan, the grandfather of one of today's firemen, Joe Eskridge. (Courtesy of the Sea Bright Fire Department.)

The Ladies Auxiliary of the Sea Bright Fire Department was organized in October 1941. Photographed are the members of the auxiliary at an installation dinner. Shown on the right, seated fourth from the front is councilwoman and mayor-elect Maria Fernandes, with her mother, Adelina Fernandes. On the left seated across from Maria is Frieda Finegan, who served three times as president of the auxiliary and also as vice president, chaplain, and fund-raiser for the First Aid Squad Auxiliary. Two seats to the left of Finegan is former councilwoman, teacher, and author Joan Burealey. At Christmas, the auxiliary gives $100 to the New Jersey Fireman's Home in Boonton.

This 1900 photograph shows a blacksmith shop, a G. G. Heidl Jr. bakery trunk, and other shops on East Ocean Avenue. None of these stores exist today on Ocean Avenue. (Courtesy of the Sea Bright Fire Department.)

This is the sign of the Sea Bright Police Department, founded in 1896, which stands alongside the Sea Bright Fire Department and Sea Bright Rescue Squad on Ocean Avenue.

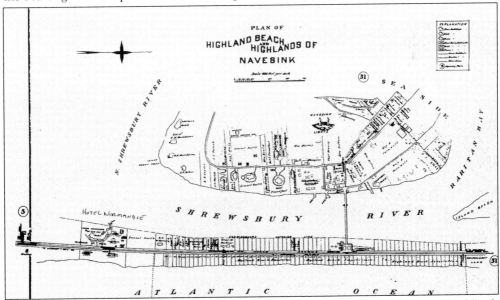

This early-20th-century plan shows Highland Beach, once a section of Sea Bright, and Highlands of Navesink. Note on the plan the Navesink Lights, which are now known as the Twin Lights of the Highlands; they overlook the Shrewsbury River and the Normandie Hotel, which was one of Sea Bright's most famous hotels. (Courtesy of the Monmouth Beach Cultural Center.)

This *c.* 1910 photograph of Sea Bright fishermen shows sidewalks that were actually dipped, so nets and carts with fish and also equipment could be brought in and stored in sheds.

Heroic Sea Bright firemen are shown putting out the fire of the Hotel Pannaci on October 31, 1953—so fell a Sea Bright landmark. The building on the right, the Charles Manor, was also damaged by the fire. (Courtesy of Monmouth County historian George H. Moss Jr.)

This is another image of the Sea Bright Fire Department putting out the fire on the night of October 31, 1953, that destroyed the Charles Manor, which was a very famous Sea Bright landmark. (Courtesy of Daniel Hennessey.)

Another Halloween tragedy falls on Sea Bright. This time, more than 25 years later, a terrible storm struck this sunny summertime town. Shown is a photograph as the ocean poured over the seawall like an angry Niagara Falls, flooding Ocean Avenue. (Courtesy of Adelina Fernandes.)

Adelina Fernandes, whose home is on Ocean Avenue, stands in front of her house as she looks at the devastation created by a "Halloween storm." (Courtesy of Adelina Fernandes.)

This 1940 photograph shows the Sea Bright Fire Department giving a demonstration at the Sea Bright School of how to escape from the building should a fire occur. (Courtesy the Sea Bright Fire Department.)

The heroism of Sea Bright Fire Department members is evident as they put out a fire. Sea Bright has had its share of tragic fire, and the fire department has always performed a class act for the residents of its town. (Courtesy of Daniel Hennessey.)

This is a 1948 aerial photograph of Sea Bright. Ocean Avenue and a hotel, the Peninsula House Hotel, are visible. Also take notice of the Sea Bright Bridge and some of the nearby town of Rumson. (Courtesy of Monmouth County historian George H. Moss Jr.)

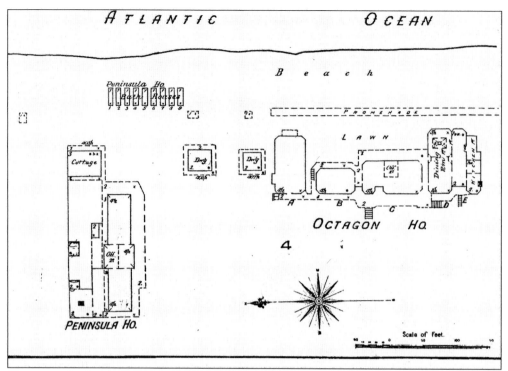

Shown is a Sea Bright 1886 map drawn up by the Sanborn Map Company depicting three of Sea Bright's famous landmarks, the Peninsula House Hotel, Peninsula House Bath Houses, and the Octagon Hotel. (Courtesy of Monmouth County historian George H. Moss Jr.)

In *The New Jersey Coast and Pines* by Gustav Kobbe (1889), the reader is shown images of life as depicted in Nauvoo and Galilee, which are two sections of what was later to become simply known as Sea Bright. (Courtesy of the Thomas Varne Museum and Library.)

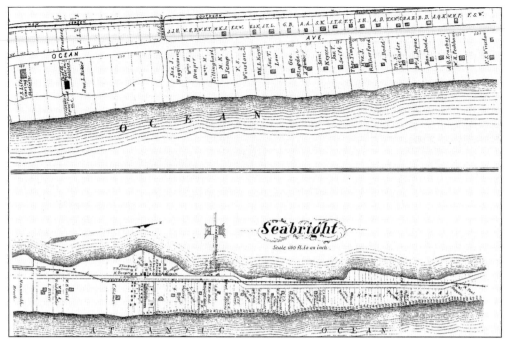

An 1878 map of Sea Bright coast, published by Woolman and Boose of Philadelphia, shows the rows and rows of "cottagers" that lined Ocean Avenue and the coastline. (Courtesy of the Atlantic Highlands Historical Society.)

After a long day of fishing, fishermen, pictured here around 1910, come in to shore to rest their boat on the Sea Bright beach. (Courtesy of Daniel Hennessey.)

This horrific photograph of the 1914 storm that devastated Sea Bright is a close-up of the intensity of the storm's destruction and shows houses literally torn to pieces. (Courtesy of Daniel Hennessey.)

The people atop the rocks inspect damage after another storm that hit hard along the Sea Bright coastline; luckily this "cottager" home remained intact. (Courtesy of Daniel Hennessey.)

This is an aerial photograph of the 1914 storm that shows the destruction surrounding this "cottager" home. The vast openness of the waters of the Atlantic Ocean is intimidating, as is the power of its strength when it becomes enraged. (Courtesy of Daniel Hennessey.)

Shown is a photograph during Sea Bright's beach replenishment, which made Sea Bright's beaches just as beautiful as they were for so many decades. (Courtesy of Adelina Fernandes.)

The image above shows May Day at the Sea Bright School and the children as they dance around the May Day pole. The Sea Bright School was located on River Street; the school was built in 1882 and remained attended by Sea Bright residents until around 1995. Shown below is another photograph of children at the Sea Bright School enjoying games on May Day.

Last Days for payment without interest charges 6% **Aug. 1st** for Third Quarter **Nov. 1st** for Fourth Quarter	**1 9 4 9 T A X E S** **FINAL BILL** Third and Fourth Quarters **BOROUGH OF SEA BRIGHT** Monmouth County, New Jersey EDMUND W. CLINE, Collector 13 CHURCH STREET Tel. Sea Bright 2-0684 ARTHUR O. AXELSEN, Assessor.	**TAX RATE** PER $100.00 County Tax Rate $1.49640667 Library Tax .02965290 Dis. School Tax 3.80724965 Municipal Tax 2.95509991 $7.31894147

Mr. Ovid C Bianchi
327 Main Street
Orange, NJ

FOLIO 19

To BOROUGH OF SEA BRIGHT, Dr.

For the annual Tax for the Year 1949 Assessed for State, County and Local Purposes.
See Explanation of New Tax Law on Reverse Side of This Bill.

Description of Property Taxed.		Assessed Valuation	**3rd Quarter**
Block No. 17 Lot. No. 18. 14 of 47B		$6,280	DUE AUGUST 1st, 1949
Land 2,280 Buildings 4000			Amount - $138.11
			Interest and Costs $
Personal Property - - -	$	250	Total - $
Total Valuation Real and Personal Property	$		
Deductions and Exemptions - -	$		**4th Quarter**
Net Valuation - - -	$	6,530	
			DUE NOVEMBER 1st, 1949
Amount of Tax—Real and Personal -	$	510.54	Amount - $138.11
Amount Billed 1st and 2nd Quarters -	$	234.32	
Balance Due Second Half 1949 - -	$	276.22	Interest and Costs $
			Total - $

PAYMENTS

3rd Quarter Payment	4th Quarter Payment
Received on July 27, 1949 Edmund W. Cline Collector.	Received on Oct 1, 1949 Edmund W. Cline Collector.

Shown is a copy of the 1949 final tax bill for the Borough of Sea Bright in Monmouth County for the third and fourth quarters sent to commissioner Ovid C. Bianchi on 327 Main Street, in Orange. He owned a summer residence on Ocean Avenue in the North Beach section of Sea Bright.

Pictured is a copy of a July 21, 1908, will of Euphemia A. Hawes to her son James Anderson Hawes. He did sell the said real estate property, which was located on Ocean Avenue, to William F. Pettes. The property at that time was said to be in the Normandie section of Sea Bright. Today is considered to be in the North Beach section.

James Anderson Hawes, Ind. and as Executor of the City, County and State of New York et al

-To-

William F. Pettes of the same place

: AGREEMENT
: Book 831 page 157
: Dated July 14, 1908
: Ackgd. July 14, 1908
: Rec'd July 21, 1908

Whereas, by the Will of the late Euphemia A. Hawes, an exemplified copy of which will is recorded in the Office of the Clerk of Monmouth County, Book S-2 of Wills, page 425, a trust is created in the sum of $20,000. for the benefit of her son, James Anderson Hawes and others and it is provided that it may be agreed between the executor or executors and the trustee or trustees therein named to select some certain pierce of real estate belonging to the said deceased in lieu of cash and the balance of the estate is left absolutely to the said James Anderson Hawes, except as to three small specific gifts or legacies, and

Whereas, James Anderson Hawes, Individually and as Executor has contracted with William F. Pettes to sell a certain piece of property with the house thereon erected formerly belonging to the late Euphemia A. Hawes at Normandie in the State of New Jersey and is about to convey the said property and

Whereas, the said property at Normandie, N.J. has not been selected as part of said Trust estate and the Executor has not made his accounting and the Trust has not been created out of the entire estate and therefore, those names in the said Will as trustees have acquired no interest in the said property of any kind whatsoever.

NOW THIS AGREEMENT WITNESSETH, that James Anderson

Sea Bright inventor Frank Perez, shown here around 1950, patented and created the Perez Reel, a fishing reel used for saltwater surf casting, squidding, bottom fishing, and trolling. The reel was handmade, which meant that all the parts were precisely fitted by hand; Perez is shown in front of his car in Sea Bright.

This photograph shows Sea Bright in an undated storm along Ocean Avenue. Notice how the entire street would become another part of the ocean and river, which would come together during such a storm. (Courtesy of the Sea Bright Fire Department.)

Sea Bright was struck by another act of Mother Nature on March 6, 1962, which devastated both Monmouth and Ocean Counties. Shown here is the North Beach section of Ocean Avenue.

In 1960, the infamous Hurricane Donna shook and damaged Sea Bright and the surrounding area. Sandy Hook can be seen in this photograph from Ocean Avenue.

This photograph was taken after the "storm of the century" in December 1992, on Ocean Avenue, which was at the time the residence of Marie H. Brown, the mother of the owner of this photograph. There used to be a cement protection wall in front and alongside the home that the storm took down and knocked out from the foundation.

The house next door to the former residence of Brown was also seriously damaged in the front of the home. Brown was taken out of her home by rowboat, as told by her granddaughter Nancy Brown Burchardt. Brown passed away the following year.

Shown are both the Peninsula House Hotel and the Sea Bright Beach Club in the background. What is very interesting about this c. 1955 photograph is the large beach with no snow fences and dunes that exist today. (Courtesy of Daniel Hennessey.)

This photograph shows the Sea Bright beach during the replenishment work. What is interesting about this photograph is how the ocean forms sandbars. During the replenishment, sandbars would form with sand dollars and starfish. The ocean would be very clean and welcoming. (Photograph by Ann Early.)

Shown at the moment it happened is the ocean overflowing the seawall on Sandpiper Lane during the "storm of the century," which damaged much of the street and the surrounding area.

This photograph shows another area of the seawall that the ocean destroyed and the sidewalk areas of the street during this terrible nor'easter storm that impacted most of Monmouth County.

Shown is another image of sidewalk destruction from this devastating "storm of the century" that is still talked about to the present day.

A nearby marina feels the same pain as boats were torn apart, as happened with several marinas in Sea Bright as a result of the storm.

The "storm of the century" also destroyed the docks where many boats were housed.

Shown is a photograph (around 1910) of the U.S. Coast Guard coming onto the beach of Sea Bright with a fishing boat. (Courtesy of Daniel Hennessey.)

This photograph (also around 1910) shows the U.S. Coast Guard having come to the Sea Bright shore with one of its fishing boats. (Courtesy of Daniel Hennessey.)

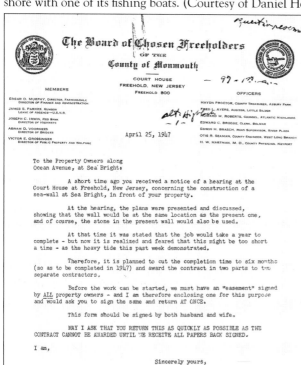

This is an April 25, 1947, document from county counsel Howard W. Roberts to the property owners along Ocean Avenue concerning the construction of a seawall along Ocean Avenue, which would be constructed in front of the property owners' homes.

Two

THE PLACE TO BE BY THE SEA

If ever there was a seaside town to vacation, Sea Bright is the town to enjoy oneself in the good old summertime.

In this chapter are pictures of the greatest place to be by the sea. For decades, Sea Bright was a resort town with some of the most luxurious hotels and restaurants to be found on the eastern seacoast. For instance, in 1875, George B. Sandt, president of the Sea Bright National Bank, built the Octagon Hotel that opened for its guests in the summer of 1876, and in 1887, Edward Pannaci came to Sea Bright and later opened the Hotel Pannaci, which became known as the "Delmonico of Sea Bright." There was also the Sea Bright Inn, the Normandie-by-the-Sea, and the Peninsula House Hotel. Today residents and visitors to Sea Bright can enjoy the Fairbanks Inn Resort and Marina, McCloone's Rum Runner, Harry's Lobster House, and Donovan's Reef Restaurant. There were, and still remain, beach clubs along Ocean Avenue that vacationers throughout the years have enjoyed, such as the Sea Bright Beach Club, the New Chapel Beach Club, the Tradewinds Beach Club, and the Driftwood Beach Club. Sea Bright has many marinas for those who want to dock their boat and ride them along the Shrewsbury and Navesink Rivers. The Ocean View Marina and the Fairbanks Inn Resort and Marina are just two that one can find along Ocean Avenue.

Sea Bright also enjoys the artistic life where residents can enjoy viewing and buying the picturesque and beautiful paintings of artist Lois Sommers, who for many years has displayed her paintings of Sea Bright and the surrounding area along Ocean Avenue.

This 1895 aerial by W. Louis Sonntag is titled "Overlooking the Course of the International Yacht-Races from the Highland Light-House" and depicts the yacht races from Sandy Hook Bay entering Highland Beach (now Sea Bright) into the Shrewsbury River. Notice the old drawbridge that brought travelers into what is today known as Sea Bright. Sea Bright has been known for its boat races as early as 1789.

The Hotel Pannaci was located on Ocean Avenue and was one of Sea Bright's most famous landmarks. Edward Pannaci came to Sea Bright in 1887, and by 1900, he owned an entire block of real estate holdings. The Hotel Pannaci was a household word among the millionaire circles and was known as the "Delmonico of Sea Bright." (Courtesy of Daniel Hennessey.)

Sea Bright Hardware, otherwise known as "Fowler's," was located on Ocean Avenue. As a child, the author would often go with her parents to the store, where she found the proprietors to be very warm and friendly. (Courtesy of Daniel Hennessey.)

Pictured here is the Sea Bright School graduating class of 1946. Some of the graduates pictured are Millie Kube (front row at left), who later served as treasurer and sunshine person for the Ladies Auxiliary of the Sea Bright Fire Department; Anna Marie Bayer, the daughter of the former chief of police; and former borough clerk Pat Dougherty (front row at right). The famous Peninsula House Hotel can be seen in the background.

This young lady is about to test the water of the Shrewsbury River on a great summer day in 1956. Notice the Twin Lights in the background across the Shrewsbury River.

This is a 1946 postcard of the Sea Bright Yacht Club, which was located on Ocean Avenue. Today the yacht club does not exist, and it is now a private residence.

This Ocean Avenue family seems to be enjoying a beautiful summer day on the beach in 1953.

This wood engraving by Granville Perkins is titled *The Stranded Steamship "L'Amerique" at Sea Bright*. Perkins recorded, this very cold January morning, the breeches buoy rescue of a passenger from the grounded transatlantic steamship *L'Amerique*. Both the rescuers and those rescued huddled by a warming fire as the United States Life Saving Service came to help them. A group of French nuns that were en route to the Midwest were among the 216 passengers and crew saved.

This wood engraving, titled *A Scene on the Fishing Banks Off Sea Bright, New Jersey — A Chip Off the Old Block*, is from an unknown artist. The etching shows a proud grandfather as he watches the startled young fisherman as his catch leaps from the sea. In the distance are commercial party boats from New York, fishing off the banks of Sea Bright.

In this 1920 photograph, Sea Bright resident Lance Rodgers holds a huge fish in front of the United Methodist Church of Sea Bright (left), Sea Bright Police Station (middle), and Fowler's hardware store (partially seen to the right). (Courtesy of the Sea Bright Fire Department, photograph by David Hillthal.)

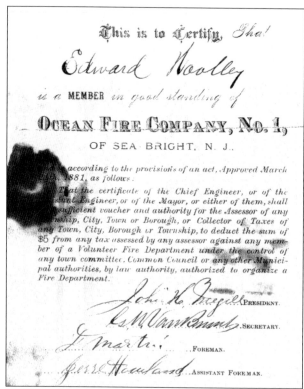

A certificate of the Ocean Fire Company No. 1 of Sea Bright certifies that Edward Woolley is a member of good standing, and it is signed by president John H. Megill, secretary C. S. M. Van Brunt, foreman L. Martin, and assistant foreman Jerre Howland. (Courtesy of the Sea Bright Fire Department.)

This photograph taken around 1950 shows members of the Sea Bright Fire Department at the fire station after a parade. Notice the trophy that the fire department received at the event. (Courtesy of the Sea Bright Fire Department.)

This October 1, 1978, photograph is of the Sea Bright Fire Department's winning field team. (Courtesy of the Sea Bright Fire Department.)

The popular Peninsula House Hotel is shown during the 1930s in this spectacular postcard "Peninsula House (Directly on the Ocean) — Sea Bright, New Jersey." The Peninsula House Hotel was one of Sea Bright's most famous hotels and landmarks.

This November 7, 1891, sketch by M. J. Burns, titled *Fisherman Landing In Surf, Sea Bright*, was shown in *Harper's Weekly*. It shows women coming out to meet their husbands after a day's fishing. (Courtesy of the Monmouth Beach Cultural Center.)

The Normandie Hotel
Normandie by the Sea, Seabright, N.J., c. 1909

This 1901 postcard of the Normandie Hotel, or Normandie-by-the-Sea, in Sea Bright shows the hotel located by the depot of Long Branch and Sea Bright Railroad with the Shrewsbury River seen behind the hotel. A fire in the early 1900s destroyed the Normandie Hotel. (Courtesy of the Monmouth Beach Cultural Center, artwork by Richard Sass.)

The Fairbanks Inn Resort and Marina has been enjoyed by tourists for more than 30 years. It is located on Ocean Avenue, and the marina sits on the beautiful Shrewsbury River. (Courtesy of the Fairbanks Inn Resort and Marina.)

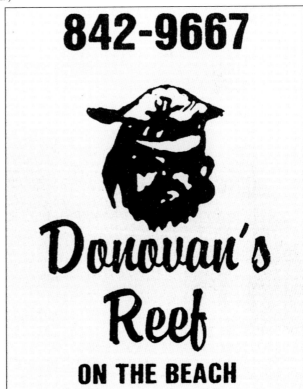

Pictured is a pack of matches advertising Donovan's Reef on the Beach, located on Ocean Avenue in the center of Sea Bright, which is an immensely popular restaurant and nightspot for the residents of Sea Bright and the surrounding area.

On August 29, 1912, at 3:30 p.m., Ethel wrote to J. M. Line of 144 Centre Street in Carbonler, Pennsylvania, on the back of this postcard labeled "Octagon Hotel, Sea Bright, N.J.": "Beautiful ride, but hands are too cold to write. Ethel." Note the railroad tracks in front of the Octagon Hotel.

McCloone's Rum Runner is one of Sea Bright's most popular restaurants. Located on Ocean Avenue and overlooking the Shrewsbury River, McCloone's Rum Runner was purchased on New Year's Eve 1986 by Tim McCloone. It opened in October 1987. Residents in the surrounding area of Sea Bright enjoy the cuisine and the beautiful dining experience overlooking the Shrewsbury River. (Courtesy of McCloone's Rum Runner.)

For 50 years, the Driftwood Beach Club has been one of Sea Bright's most popular beach clubs. Shown is a 1960s aerial view of the beach club along Ocean Avenue. The back of the postcard describes the club as "Jersey's Complete Resort." (Courtesy of the Driftwood Beach Club.)

Carol Wilson is pictured on the left of this photograph. His father, Frank Otterstrom, emigrated from Sweden (around 1882, the name Otterstrom was changed to Wilson). Sea Bright was settled by Scandinavians. Wilson was a war hero who served in the U.S. Army during World War I. He is shown here in 1917 with a fellow Holy Cross basketball teammate.

Carol Wilson is shown in this photograph around 1915, holding a Holy Cross basketball as a member of the Holy Cross basketball team.

Every town has its share of war heroes, and Sea Bright is no exception. Shown here are three World War I heroes (around 1917); in the center is Wilson.

On a beautiful day in the summer of 1918, Carol and Mae Wilson (pictured to the right in the front row) enjoy the beach with fellow Sea Bright sunbathers.

The Holy Cross basketball team enjoys a summer day on the beach around 1918. Pictured third from the left in the front row is Carol Wilson.

Another day at the beach shows Mae Wilson with friends and an unidentified Sea Bright serviceman, having a great time.

Wilson (left) and a friend pull a cart with passengers, who are very much enjoying the ride. Note in the background the fishing boats stationed on the Sea Bright beach.

This is a postcard of the popular Gaiter's Bar and Grill located on Ocean Avenue nestled between the Shrewsbury River and the Atlantic Ocean. Gaiter's Bar and Grill has been a part of Sea Bright dining for more than 30 years. It recaptures the Gatsby era with its decor, cuisine, and fine wines. (Courtesy of Gaiter's Bar and Grill.)

Sea Bright's famous Harry's Lobster House, first established in 1920, is located on Ocean Avenue. Tourists and residents alike have enjoyed Harry's Lobster House seafood for decades.

Sea Bright has always had a sense of humor. This postcard, dated around 1920 and showing the caption "What I saw through — the Keyhole in Sea Bright, N. J.," is very creative. (Courtesy of Monmouth County historian George H. Moss Jr.)

This postcard typifies life in the 1920s in summertime Sea Bright and has the caption "Buffet Luncheon on Boardwalk — Peninsula House — Sea Bright, New Jersey." (Courtesy of Monmouth County historian George H. Moss Jr.)

This is a 1900 drawing of the Sea Bright Inn. The Sea Bright Bridge is located in the area where the Sea Bright Inn used to stand. (Courtesy of Monmouth County historian George H. Moss Jr.)

Harmony Hall,

Seabright,

AUGUST 18, 1882.

Programme.

PLOT FOR PLOT.

—

CAPTAIN HARCOURT.
MISS FLORENCE LESLIE.

—

SCENE:
DRAWING ROOM IN A COUNTRY HOUSE.

To be followed by the One-Act Comedietta,

Little Sentinel.

Characters:

Mistress LETTY HAWTHORN, - Proprietress of the Farm.
MAY, - - - - The Little Sentinel.
Mr. WEEDLETON COAXER, - An elderly " Lady Killer."
Capt. CLARENCE COURTINGTON, - Of the Dragoons.
SIM, - - - - - A Young Farmer.

SCENE:

Before the Peninsula House Hotel, the building was Harmony Hall. Shown is an August 18, 1882, program for both a play titled *Plot for Plot* and the one-act comedietta *Little Sentinel*. (Courtesy of Monmouth County historian George H. Moss Jr.)

P.-W.

MENU

———

Grape Fruit Coktail

———

Radis   Amandes Sallies   Olives

———

Consomme de Volaille en tasse

———

Homard farcis Diable

———

Mignon Filet de Boeuf   Sauce Champignons

Pommes Parisienne Persillade

Petit pois a la Francaise

———

Waldorf Salade

Glace de Fantasie

Gateaux Assortis

Cafe

HOTEL PANNACI
Thursday, April 28, 1921

Pictured here is a Hotel Pannaci French cuisine dinner menu for Thursday, April 28, 1921. (Courtesy of Monmouth County historian George H. Moss Jr.)

Telephone 53 Sea Bright

Edward Pannaci

Sea Bright, N. J.

Real Estate, Loans, Insurance.

I have in my charge, on the Rumson Road, Sea Bright, Monmouth Beach, Low Moor, Highlands, of Navesink, Long Branch, Elberon, Deal and Allenhurst, Furnished Cottages for Rent and for Sale.

Renting prices from $500 to $7,500.

HOTEL PANNACI

AND

RESTAURANT

SEA BRIGHT, N. J.

Now Open

Facing Ocean and Shrewsbury River. American and European Plans. Automobile Parties a Specialty. Rooms en suite with Baths. Special Rates for Families. Restaurant open all winter in Cottage adjoining Hotel.

Address,

Edward Pannaci, Prop.

These are two advertisements of the Hotel Pannaci and Restaurant. The first advertisement describes Edward Pannaci's business of "Real Estate, Loans, and Insurance," and the second advertisement gives a description of the famous Pannaci Restaurant. (Courtesy of Monmouth County historian George H. Moss Jr.)

Shown in this photograph is the front of the Tradewinds Beach Club. The Tradewinds Beach Club was one of Sea Bright's most well-known beach clubs, located on Ocean Avenue for almost 50 years until it was demolished in 2003. (Courtesy of Barbara Thornberry Photography.)

Pictured are the Seabright Bowl trophies (around 1900) of the Sea Bright Lawn Tennis and Cricket Club, a popular club at the beginning of the 20th century. (Courtesy of the Monmouth County Historical Association Library and Archives.)

Halloween is a very important holiday in Sea Bright. Pictured is one of the store windows that Sea Bright children would decorate for this scary holiday.

Also pictured is another window decorated by the children of Sea Bright. For many years, a man on a bicycle would ride by and judge the window drawings.

This photograph is of Paddy Miller, Miss Sea Bright 1955, bathing on the Sea Bright beach. Miller is also a former president of the Sea Bright Ladies Auxiliary.

Chris's Landing
On Route 36 — Ocean Ave.
Sea Bright, N. J.

Shown is a postcard of Chris's Landing. On the back of this postcard, Chris's Landing "invites you to a real enjoyable day FISHING, CRABBING, CRUISING on the beautiful SHREWSBURY RIVER. Fishing the Year Round! 100 new rowboats, $1.50 per day. Bait, Tackle, Luncheonette, Boat Storage. Outboards to Rent. Free Towing. Parking. Reservation Phone CHRIS, Sea Bright 2-0281." The unknown sender of this postcard wrote to John Gulash, 3rd of 238 Sherman Street in Perth Amboy, "FLOUNDERS & EELS ARE IN!!!!" Today Chris's Landing is no longer in existence; it was demolished some years ago and was replaced by condominiums and townhouses.

Three unidentified members of the Sea Bright First Aid Squad, around 1945, are relaxing with a game of checkers and having a good time. (Courtesy of the Sea Bright Fire Department.)

In August 1961, Jimmy Cousins poses with his fish, along the dock in his backyard. In the background, his father (left) and Charlie Massina, his next-door neighbor, look on.

William Matthew Cousins, a native of Sea Bright, is seen here in 1953 after a day of fishing, in front of his house on Normandie Place with brother William Jr.

This photograph features the "Beach Boys," friends of Sea Bright native Jimmy Cousins's grandfather Foley Cousins, as they spend the day on the beach in the 1920s.

These friends are really enjoying a great day on the beach. It was "the way they were" back in footloose and fancy-free 1929.

Foley Cousins (grandfather of Jimmy Counsins) and friends have a great time on the Sea Bright beach around 1929, on a one of those lazy, hazy, crazy days of summer.

Taken around 1900, this image of a stylish Sea Bright lady, an unidentified friend of Jimmy Cousins's grandparents, captures a moment and an age long gone.

These two women pose for a photograph on a dock in the backyard of Jimmy Cousins's grandparents' home in the 1920s with the beautiful Shrewsbury River in the background.

Five ladies and a gentleman on a dock strike a pose around 1910, with the Shrewsbury River shown again in the background.

The Blue Water Inn on Ocean Avenue opened up in the spring of 1975 as a small restaurant. Shown in this photograph are its owner Mike Bivona and his wife, Tina, enjoying a conversation with jazz great Johnny Hartman at the club. The Bivonas turned it into one of Sea Bright's most popular jazz clubs and restaurants. It featured many jazz musicians, such as Tal Farlow, a Sea Bright resident who also played with Jack Six on the Bass, and Warren Chaisson of the Vibes, Paul Quinichette, and Artie Miller.

Photographed is Johnny Hartman singing at the Blue Water Inn. Hartman was born in Chicago and became a popular jazz ballad singer in the 1940s and 1950s. He made his first LP in 1956. The Grammy-nominated singer often performed at the Blue Water Inn.

The great jazz guitarist Tal Farlow was a resident of Sea Bright from 1958 until his death in July 1998. Farlow was compared to Charlie Parker for his speed but was a smooth and relaxed player. Farlow played with Artie Shaw, Mirt Jackson, Red Norvo, and Charlie Minegus. He is seen in this photograph on the deck of his waterfront home in Sea Bright playing his guitar. (Photograph by John Cowie.)

Farlow is at work here, sign painting the boat *Fat Chance* in 1981. When Farlow moved to Sea Bright, he played around locally and also worked as a sign painter. (Courtesy of Lorenzo de Stefano/Productions A-Propos.)

In 1981, Farlow gave an informal performance at his home in Sea Bright. He was one of the greats of jazz. (Courtesy of Lorenzo de Stefano/Productions A-Propos.)

For many years, Tina Kearny has vacationed in Sea Bright. Seen here, she enjoys a beautiful day with her boxer pup Mick at Atlantic Way in Sea Bright.

"Beach buddies" Jeanne Gough (left) and Tina Kearny are pictured having a great time at the beach by Donovan's Reef, a popular restaurant and bar on Ocean Avenue.

Photographer and Sea Bright summer resident Ann Early (center) is seen here with "the gang" on the old jetty. High tide on the "Baby Beach" is seen in the background. Ann Early says, "We came from New York, New Jersey and gathered every summer to bathe and sun and get reacquainted. People have moved on and gone, but we have such happy memories." (Courtesy of Ann Early.)

Jared Gough, grandson of Jeanne Gough, competed and won in the third annual Sea Bright Skim Bash. Jared holds the award in his right hand.

From left to right, Lion, Jared, and Kelsey Gough seem to be having a great time in the summertime on the seawall in front of Gaiter's Bar and Grill (in the background).

Barbara Markey Pasko, shown in this photograph (third child in line), enjoyed summers in Sea Bright. She recalls, "I remember Sea Bright as a little girl. We went to a place under big rocks and changed into bathing suits. The ocean was great. My dad tied ropes around our waist and took us out onto the waves as he held onto the rope. It was a great place, and Mom brought peaches, sandwiches, and milk for us to each lunch. Those were the days." It is so wonderful to read memories of someone who enjoyed Sea Bright so much.

This postcard, titled "Ocean Bathing Highland Beach, N. J.," shows bathers enjoying themselves during a day at the beach. On August 31, 1906, Geraldine wrote to her aunt at 44 Seventh Avenue, Brooklyn, "Dear Aunt I am all sun-burnt. It is a grand place down here. From Geraldine."

Titled "The Boardwalk, Highland Beach, N. J.," this postcard shows summertime at the shore in the early 20th century. In the background is one of Sea Bright's train stations. There were a total of four train stations.

This is a scene looking across at Sea Bright from the Highlands. This postcard, dated September 5, 1921, and titled "Scene on the Shrewsbury River from the East View Hotel, Highlands, N.J.," was sent to Elenor Barlow of 7920 Constance Avenue, Chicago. It says, "How are you wish you were with me. Aunty Katherine."

This May 1959 photograph of two young girls on a dock along the Shrewsbury River shows the entrance of the Navesink River in the background.

These three youngsters are really enjoying a Sea Bright summer day in 1955, swimming in the waters of the Shrewsbury River.

Noreen is having a great time taking pictures of everyone on the Sea Bright beach as her two brothers in the background enjoy a good swim in the water. In the distant background is one of Sea Bright's most noted landmarks, the Peninsula House Hotel. Notice how large and wide the Sea Bright beach was before the snow fences and dunes were installed many years later.

Cynthia Bianchi sunbathes in the backyard of her family's summer home on Ocean Avenue. Notice how overgrown and rather rural Sea Bright still was at this time in 1947. In the background are the Shrewsbury River and the entrance to the Navesink River.

This couple is enjoying a day on the beach around 1947. Take notice of how in the background the rocks of the seawall are separated from one another; they were not at this time cemented together.

Young Stephen Dolce looks as though he is about to get into this rowboat and ride along the Shrewsbury River (around 1947). Notice in the background the "cottager" homes that lined the North Beach section of Ocean Avenue.

Little Robyn Bianchi is having fun on the Sea Bright beach with her sister Cynthia behind her, on a beautiful summer day in 1949.

Sea Barn

Swimming at Private Ocean and River Beaches Boating and fishing Delightfully cool rooms rented by Day, Week or Season

Todino's owner, mgr.

270 Ocean Ave, Sea Bright, N.J.

Sea Bright 2-0685

This *c.* 1950 postcard of the Sea Barn Hotel Restaurant and Bar was very popular in its day. Gertrude Ederle, who was the first woman to swim the English Channel, trained in the Highlands and Sea Bright and also stayed at the Sea Barn Hotel Restaurant and Bar. The Sea Barn Hotel Restaurant and Bar (around 1950) became the Ocean Spray Marina, then in 1971, it was renamed the Ocean View Marina.

This postcard speaks for itself: "Bathing in the Shrewsbury River, Highland Beach, N. J." It was sent to Eva Paton by Netrie, with no address on it. Netrie simply wrote to Eva, "Come on in the water is fine Netrie."

The Surf House was a popular restaurant in Highland Beach. Minnie wrote to Elsie Gruber of 84½ East Jersey Street, Elizabeth, on July 6, 1900, "We are at Highland Beach and having a fine time. There was a terrible wind storm on the water and the boats rocked like a good fellow. Will tell you more when I see you. Minnie."

Shown in this photograph is the artwork of noted Monmouth County artist Lois Sommers, who has frequently displayed her artwork upon the gate of the United Methodist Church of Sea Bright along Ocean Avenue. Sommers has painted many portraits over the years of the Jersey Shore, such as the Sandy Hook Lighthouse and the Twin Lights of the Highlands, which can be seen in this photograph.

This is a backyard view of the Tradewinds Beach Club, which is located on Ocean Avenue. Notice how both the beach and the seawall come very close to the beach club to protect it from storms. (Courtesy of Barbara Thornberry Photography.)

Lovebirds Carol and Mae Wilson are enjoying themselves very much on a spectacular summer day on the beautiful Sea Bright beach in 1920.

The Peninsula House Hotel was the most famous and popular hotel on the New Jersey shore for many decades. Two streets in the back of the hotel were destroyed in one of Sea Bright's storms. The Peninsula House Hotel was destroyed by a fire in 1986. Today a parking lot is there. (Courtesy of Daniel Hennessey.)

Three

BEAUTIFUL SEA BRIGHT

This chapter is appropriately titled "Beautiful Sea Bright," for it is filled with picturesque images. Seen in this chapter are images from the collection of Daniel Hennessey and photographers Ann Early, Lola Adolf, and Eleanor Milland, who all captured the beauty and charm of Sea Bright with the lens. The magnificent mansions that lined Ocean Avenue in the late 19th century and through much of the 20th century were called "cottages," built by wealthy businessmen who became known as "cottagers." There were four sections of Sea Bright—Normandie, North Beach, Low Moor, and Galilee—and beautiful homes could be found in each of these areas. The United Methodist Church of Sea Bright and the Presbyterian Chapel both graced Ocean Avenue, which can be seen in photographs in this chapter. Today only the United Methodist Church remains. The beauty of the Shrewsbury and Navesink Rivers was captured in many photographs and postcards. Sea Bright will always stand in beauty.

Shown is a winter photograph of the United Methodist Church of Sea Bright on Ocean Avenue. The church was founded in 1865. There was a fire in the late 1800s. The church was rebuilt in 1893. Today part of the church is E. F. Mason Insurance, established in 1978. Robert J. Long is pastor of the church. (Courtesy of Daniel Hennessey.)

A photograph of another beautiful church in Sea Bright, the Presbyterian Chapel, is located on Ocean Avenue. The Presbyterian Chapel does not exist today. (Courtesy of Daniel Hennessey.)

Everyone wanted to have a home in Sea Bright, notably tobacco heiress Doris Duke. In this photograph, a mansion for Duke is being built in April 1927. (Courtesy of Daniel Hennessey.)

A photograph of another "cottager" is that of the summer residence of Washington E. Connor, also in the North Beach section of Sea Bright on Ocean Avenue. Connor bought many properties in Sea Bright and, in fact, was one of the largest owners of real estate in Sea Bright. (Courtesy of Daniel Hennessey.)

Wells Cottage, on Ocean Avenue, was the residence of D. B. Keeler Jr. (Courtesy of Daniel Hennessey.)

Seabright. N.J. R.R. Station.

This October 27, 1910, postcard, simply titled "Seabright, N.J., R.R. Station," captures the Gilded Age in Sea Bright. Ethel Stanton of Pedrickton received the postcard, which plainly says, "Lovingly Miss Turner."

This enchanting photograph shows the home of John L. Riker, another wealthy "cottager," on Ocean Avenue in Sea Bright. (Courtesy of Daniel Hennessey.)

Shown is a 1946 photograph of the summer residence of former mayor and commissioner of Orange Ovid C. Bianchi, located on Ocean Avenue in the North Beach section of Sea Bright.

This genteel postcard, titled "Mary Patten Boat up Shrewsbury River, Sea Bright, N.J.," captures the beauty of the *Mary Patten* along the Shrewsbury River as it passes by the beautiful oceanfront cottages.

On July 5, 1935, this postcard titled "Scene on Shrewsbury River, Sea Bright, N. J." shows just how beautiful the Shrewsbury River is on a serene summer day. The back of the postcard reads, "We are having a fine time. Hope all are well. Love Lou & Beat & Family." It was sent to a Mr. and Mrs. J. Hlisch at 477 Catherine Street, Fort Lee.

Bridge over Shrewsbury River at Highlands, N. J.

"Bridge over Shrewsbury River at Highlands, N. J." is the title of this September 10, 1906, postcard, sent to Edy H. Arundel at 301 South Eleventh Street, New York City. "Remember this" by F. H. is written on the front of the postcard. This postcard shows the Highlands Bridge going into the direction of Sea Bright, and notice the Twin Lights in the background.

This August 16, 1905, postcard titled "Draw Bridge over Shrewsbury River, Sea Bright, N.J." depicts the Sea Bright Bridge leading in the direction of Rumson. The postcard was being sent to H. Wistfall of No. 31 Lenox Road, Flatbush, Long Island. The front of the postcard reads, "The weather keeps on being beastly. We cannot stir from the piazza. I had a glorious time in town & did not return here until Monday a.m. Lots of love to you all from, Mummy."

This 1911 postcard titled "St. George's Church, Memorial to Mr. Wm. E. Strong, Seabright, N. J." was sent to Anna Bondeu of 326 North Marie Street, Fall River, Massachusetts. The sender writes to Bondeu, "We attended Church here yesterday. The sea is terrible, but we manage to keep comfortable either on the river, or in the macherie or south bay. Thank you for both of the letters. They were great. M.D."

This July 10, 1961, postcard, titled "Sea Bright, N. J.," was sent to Steve and John Truzack of 825 Parkview Terrace, Elizabeth. It says, "Hi — Hope you get this before we get to your house. Shall see you around 12 noon Monday, the weather is swell, As Ever, Helen & Bill Stoeffler." (Courtesy of Mo Cuocci.)

A beautiful "Rumson Road, Sea Bright, N. J." postcard, dated July 26, 1908, from Philadelphia, typifies one of the most breathtaking roads from Sea Bright leading into Rumson, Sea Bright's neighboring town. Miriann Morton of Elkins Park, Pennsylvania, received this postcard message reading, "West Eud., N.J. Dear Mirianny: We miss you very much. Your teddy bear is right here and sends his love to you. Have you forgotten all about big Harry? Lots of love to you & John. Affectionately, Aunt Bessie. July 26th." (Courtesy of Mo Cuocci.)

The postcard "Patten Line Steamer 'Thomas Patten' leaving Dock, Seabright, N.J." was sent on August 20, 1907, to Jessie Lewkes Linglistorvi of Dauphin County, Pennsylvania. It says, "Well I had a drive in old Ocean Avenue this morning is bright and beautiful. We are visiting New York City and will see the sights, I must say my cup of pleasure is full to the brim. Will see you more when I get home. Lovingly, Sara."

Shown is a picturesque postcard displaying the beauty of Sea Bright, and it is simply titled "Sea Bright, N.J." A Mrs. Afflebach on May 22, 1911, wrote to Mrs. E. H. Conover, 409 Fourth Avenue, in Asbury Park. It says, "Dear Mrs. C: Well we are settled once more. Hope we did not make you a lot of work by leaving all those papers behind us. Tell Marion I have a great big bed of rosies. Love to all, Mrs. Afflebach."

Beautiful Ocean Avenue of Sea Bright is seen in this picture and is the title of this August 23, 1941, postcard. It was sent to a Jean Frost of 59 Mount Airy Road in Bennardsville, New Jersey. It simply says, "Dear Jeannie, I am going to be home Wednesday come up if you aren't too busy. Love Ruthe."

This postcard, titled "Boat Landing, Highland Beach, N.J.," depicts the beautiful Shrewsbury River and the grand "cottages" that grace it. On the back of this postcard, it says, "Dear Anna We are her because we are hers. Marg." It was sent on August 25, 1908, to Anna Foley of 358 Central Avenue in Newark.

This September 1, 1937, postcard shows the new Highlands Bridge, which is the gateway to sunny Sea Bright. The description on the card could not be more accurate: "New Million Dollar Bridge from Twin Lights, Highlands, N.J." On the back of the postcard, the sender wrote, "Having a wonderful time. Enjoying the water and sunshine. Going fishing this morning. Regards, Virginia." It was sent to a Mr. and Mrs. Babick of 438 Nelson Avenue in Grantwood.

This scenic postcard, titled "Steamer 'Albertina' Coming through Draw Bridge, Highlands, N.J.," shows the ship coming from the Highlands into Sea Bright. On the back of the postcard, it is dated May 31, 1912, and simply says Harold. It was sent to Helen Meriul of Matawan.

Seen in this postcard is a beautiful aerial view of Twin Lights, as it overlooks the majestic Highlands Bridge, crossing over the Shrewsbury River into Sea Bright. The back of this c. 1935 postcard still refers to Sea Bright as Highland Beach.

What could be more scenic than a view of the Shrewsbury River in Sea Bright taken from the Twin Lights in the Highlands, with a glorious view of the Atlantic Ocean seen in the background?

Beautiful and majestic is the only way to describe this postcard (from around 1910), titled "Highlands of Navesink, N.J." It shows the Highlands Bridge as one departs the seaside town of Sea Bright.

This c. 1910 postcard titled "View from East View House, Highlands, N.J." shows the Highlands Bridge as one would enter Sea Bright crossing over the Shrewsbury River.

Tranquil and beautiful is this "Along the Shrewsbury River, Sea Bright, N.J." postcard from around 1915. The artist of this postcard expressed clearly the majesty of Sea Bright's serenity.

"Sunset on the Shrewsbury" is the name of the photograph taken by photographer Ann Early. For the last 30 years, Early has summered in the Normandie section of Sea Bright. This image, as the many shown in this chapter, captures the very beauty of Sea Bright. (Photograph by Ann Early.)

This is the Operation Sail of the tall ships, taken at the time of the nation's bicentennial in July 1976 as they ride along in glory on the Shrewsbury River. (Photograph by Ann Early.)

The breaking of the Atlantic Ocean waves along the Sea Bright beach on a sunny summer day was captured by Ann Early. The strength of the waters can be felt by the human eye. (Photograph by Ann Early.)

Early photographed the swans swimming on the Shrewsbury River in the Normandie section of Sea Bright on a tranquil summer day. Note the island in the background. One can feel euphoric looking at this scene. (Photograph by Ann Early.)

In this photograph, titled "Canoeist at Sunset," the Shrewsbury River is captured exquisitely by the shade of pink of the lantern shown in the forefront of the picture. (Photograph by Ann Early.)

Sea Bright's beaches attract interesting creatures. Ann Early's camera discovered this turtle one summer day. A friend of hers said, "They come to lay their eggs." The waters of the Atlantic Ocean have washed up to the Sea Bright shores other outstanding creatures of the water in the past. (Photograph by Ann Early.)

"Sea Bright View Across to Rumson" is the title of this photograph that depicts the beautiful Sanford White homes on the Fourth of July on the Shrewsbury River. The Shrewsbury River always brings out the spectacular beauty of those that line its waters. (Photograph by Ann Early.)

Photographed is the Sea Bright ocean beach in winter; one can feel the wintry chill but appreciate the beauty of the season. The famous architect did lots of wonderful things in this area, including the "Officer's Row" of houses on Sandy Hook. (Photograph by Ann Early.)

Seen in this photograph is the beautiful summer residence of Gen. Lewis Fitzgerald, which was another beautiful "cottage" to line Ocean Avenue in the late 1890s and the early part of the 20th century. (Courtesy of Daniel Hennessey.)

"Bird's Eye View of Rumson Road, Sea Bright, N.J." is the title of this postcard depicting another scene of beautiful Rumson Road. Chas Boneo Jr. of Sewell received a short note sent from his mother on August 10, 1929, at 9:00 a.m. saying, "Dear Son Wish you were here with us having a wonderful time From Mother & Steele."

This sailboat postcard of August 26, 1946, is quite interesting for it is written by a young girl named Louise Shelgrove to Mary Lee of Van Court, 17 Columbus Avenue, Montclair. It reads, "Hello Mary Lee, the fishing is good, the water is fine. Louise Shelgrove." It is simply expressed of how this young girl is enjoying herself in Sea Bright.

The beautiful waters of the Atlantic Ocean are caught by the camera of photographer Ann Early, and the human eye enjoys their beauty even more from the Sea Bright beaches. The ocean spewed up many things while the "buildup" of the beaches was going on; huge rusty pipes brought the sand in to build up the beaches, and treasures emerged such as sea glass and many sand dollars with special findings such as the "Father, Son, and the Holy Ghost" inside, which is said to be a lucky find. There were also rocks of many different colors, from whites, grays, beige, amber, and gold. (Photograph by Ann Early.)

Heidi the dachshund is having fun in her backyard on Normandie Place in the middle of a beautiful Sea Bright winter. The Shrewsbury River can be seen in the background.

Eleanor Milland caught with the lens of her camera the majestic waves of the waters from the Sea Bright beach. (Photograph by Eleanor Milland.)

This is a spectacular photograph of the *Sandy Hook Lady* cruising along the Shrewsbury River on a beautiful summer day. (Photograph by Ann Early.)

"Sea Bright at Dusk" shows the dock of Sea Bright resident Jimmy Cousins leading into the Shrewsbury River as it shines from the rays of the sunset.

Shown is one of the spectacular tall ships as it glides down the Shrewsbury River during the July 1976 bicentennial. (Photograph by Ann Early.)

This breathtaking photograph was taken by photographer Lola Adolf, who has photographed much of Monmouth County, from the Twin Lights in the Highlands, Sea Bright's next-door neighbor. Seen is the Highlands Bridge, which leads to the gateway of Sea Bright and the Shrewsbury River. (Photograph by Lola Adolf.)

This beautiful scene in 1930 is the picture of tranquility with the seagulls dancing in unison as the fishermen come onto shore after a long day of fishing. The magnificence of the beach is breathtaking.

The beautiful Victorian-style architecture of McCloone's Rum Runner can be seen in this photograph. A magnificent view of the Shrewsbury River can be seen by diners.

This 1927 photograph shows the "cottage" of Brainard Avery, a native of Connecticut and corporate lawyer who summered in Sea Bright with his family. Shown in the background is the "dark house," where stories were told that the king and queen lived in the house. Today the house no longer exists, and the site is now the parking lot for McCloone's Rum Runner.

The author's memories of spending summers on Ocean Avenue will last her lifetime, and compiling this book brought back those happy memories. Meeting the people of Sea Bright was both warm and fulfilling for the author.

ACROSS AMERICA, PEOPLE ARE DISCOVERING SOMETHING WONDERFUL. *THEIR HERITAGE.*

Arcadia Publishing is the leading local history publisher in the United States. With more than 3,000 titles in print and hundreds of new titles released every year, Arcadia has extensive specialized experience chronicling the history of communities and celebrating America's hidden stories, bringing to life the people, places, and events from the past. To discover the history of other communities across the nation, please visit:

www.arcadiapublishing.com

Customized search tools allow you to find regional history books about the town where you grew up, the cities where your friends and family live, the town where your parents met, or even that retirement spot you've been dreaming about.